Published by
Princeton Architectural Press
70 West 36th Street
New York, New York 10018
www.papress.com

Text © 2021 by Daisy Bird
Illustration © 2021 by Camilla Pintonato
Published by arrangement with Debbie Bibo Agency

ISBN 978-1-61689-989-9

Designer: Camilla Pintonato

For Princeton Architectural Press:
Editors: Rob Shaeffer and Kristen Hewitt
Typesetting: Paula Baver

Special thanks to Michelle Hughes, Tre Smith, "Pork" Rhyne,
and Lauren Cichocki for their invaluable feedback.

Library of Congress Control Number: 2021932406

DAISY BIRD   CAMILLA PINTONATO

PIGOLOGY

THE ULTIMATE ENCYCLOPEDIA

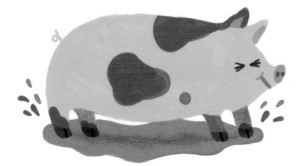

Princeton Architectural Press
New York

CONTENTS

DISCOVERING THE WORLD OF PIGS

PIGS INSIDE AND OUT

BON APPETIT!

PIGS AND HUMANS

A RAINBOW OF BREEDS

PIG PLANET

There are a billion domesticated pigs on planet Earth. That's the same as the number of people living in the United States, Russia, Japan, Egypt, Germany, the United Kingdom, Spain, Argentina, Australia, the Czech Republic, and Greece combined.

In many cultures throughout history, pigs have symbolized prosperity and security. Even today, the Chinese word for "home," 家 or *jia*, is the sign for "roof" over that for "pig." Over the centuries, we have explored different ways to keep pigs and to breed them, we have created myths and superstitions about them, and we still scatter traditional sayings about pigs throughout our conversation.

THERE ARE 51 OF US JUST ON THIS PAGE.

PIGGING OUT

Every year we eat 110,000,000 tons of pork. That's right—
ONE HUNDRED AND TEN MILLION TONS. That's the
same weight as three hundred Empire State Buildings. So it
is fair to say that pigs are pretty important to us.

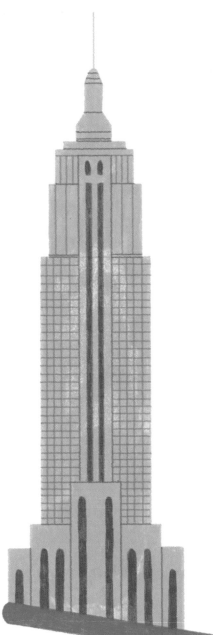

Cows give us milk, sheep give us
wool, and chickens provide eggs,
but the only reason we have ever
kept pigs is to provide us with
meat—and more pigs. This puts
them in a different category from
other livestock and has meant
that we are rather conflicted in
our feelings toward the humble
pig. We like pigs, and we find them
easy to manage and to understand,
but at the same time, we also
know that, sooner or later, every
domestic pig will end up as ham.
Or sausages. Or pork chops.
Or any of the many other delicious
foodstuffs they provide us with.
In fact, pork is the most widely
eaten meat across the globe.

1. HOT DOG
2. PORK CHOPS
3. ROAST
4. SALAMI
5. SPECK
6. MORTADELLA
7. RAW HAM
8. SAUSAGES
9. COOKED HAM

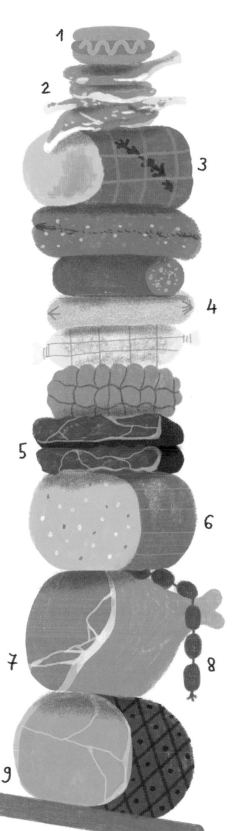

SOME VERY ANCIENT HISTORY

Long, long ago (19 to 45 million years ago, in fact), terrible-looking creatures called entelodonts roamed across North America and Eurasia. Entelodonts had slim legs, a very big, bulky body, and a long muzzle with a full set of very strong, hard teeth. Some grew as high as six feet tall. They were so fearsome that they have been nicknamed "hell pigs" or "terminator pigs." Like pigs, entelodonts were omnivorous, and they looked quite a lot like present-day wild boars. So was the entelodont the ancestor of pigs today?

A VERY ANCIENT MYSTERY

Some 19 million years ago, another creature, called the hyotherium, lived in the swamplands of central Asia. It is thought the hyotherium was an omnivore, like the entelodont, but rather smaller. Altogether, the hyotherium is a mystery. Very few fossils have been discovered, of teeth, skulls, and jaws, but they have been found in sites from Portugal to Pakistan, and there is just enough evidence to suggest that they, too, are somewhere in the modern pig's family tree.

WE ARE FAMILY (AREN'T WE?)

Technically, pigs are classed as "even-toed ungulates," which means they are related to sheep, goats, cattle, deer, antelopes, and bison. That's not so surprising, but they are also related to camels and giraffes. The pig's direct ancestor is probably the hyotherium, which evolved into the first wild boars about 2.6 million years ago. But scientists also think that the hyotherium itself is related to and descended in some way from the entelodont, which we know to have been the ancestor of hippopotamuses and even of whales and dolphins, which evolved from land animals.

GIRAFFE

PIG

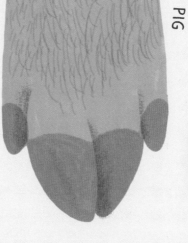

CAMEL

SHEEP

GIMME FIVE

We know pigs, camels, hippos, and giraffes (and sheep, antelopes, and bison) are related because of their feet. All these animals walk on an even number of toes—two, in the case of pigs, giraffes, and camels, four in the case of the hippo. The horse, which is an odd-toed ungulate, walks on just one toe. There are other clues to the relationship between pigs and other even-toed ungulates, such as the fact that pig and hippo teeth are ridged in the same kind of way. All these connections between different animals can now be investigated by comparing their DNA, so we know for certain which are related, and how.

HIPPOPOTAMUS

BISON

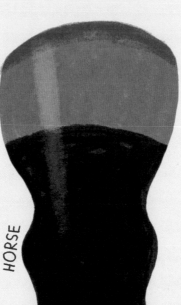

HORSE

ANTELOPE

PIGS IN THE WILD

Worldwide, there are sixteen different species of wild pig. In Africa these include the bush pig, the red river hog, warthogs, and the forest hog. Eurasia has the wild boar, which is the ancestor of all domesticated pigs today; while in Central and South America there are three different species of New World pigs, known as peccaries. There are even pigs on Pacific islands—in fact there are six separate species of them, including the warty pigs of the Philippines and the bearded pigs of Borneo.

PECCARIES

Peccaries live in herds of as many as one hundred animals. They have tusks that point down and a very pungent odor, and their favorite foods include prickly pears.

BUSH PIG

The bush pig comes from eastern and southern Africa. Males and females have a very heavy mane, which they bristle when upset.

BEARDED PIG OF BORNEO

The bearded pig not only has a splendid beard around its snout but also can grow tassels on its tail.

WARTY PIG

Male warty pigs grow a crest of hair like a Mohawk during their mating season. Warty pigs are now endangered and very rare.

GIANT FOREST HOG

The giant forest hog is the largest wild species of pig. Males weigh up to six hundred pounds and are big enough to scare off hyenas!

RAZORBACK PIG

Feral razorback pigs are descendants of domesticated pigs that escaped and bred with wild pigs. In the United States alone, it's estimated that there are six million feral pigs. They are very destructive, causing billions of dollars of damage annually.

SPOT THE DIFFERENCE

Once upon a time, all domestic pigs looked like wild boars—and would have behaved like them too. Slowly and steadily, people began to select individual animals to breed that were tamer and easier to look after. Today, at least on first glance, there are very obvious differences between wild boars and farmyard pigs.

Wild boars are covered in a thick coat of fur, usually dark in color, and males often have a noticeable ridge of tough hair standing up along their backs.

Wild boars have longer, straighter tails.

Most of a wild boar's weight and muscle are in the head and shoulders, and they have a narrower, wedge-shaped skull.

Wild boars have just nineteen vertebrae, but domesticated pigs have twenty-one to twenty-three.

Domesticated pigs generally have much less in the way of bristles, and the bristles they have are much more varied in pattern and color.

A domesticated pig may have as much as 70 percent of its weight in its hindquarters.

Domesticated pigs have shorter legs than their wild cousins.

BORN TO BE WILD

If domesticated pigs escape into the wild, within just a couple of generations they start to look more and more like wild boars. Scientists think this may be evidence that long after the earliest farmers began selecting and domesticating pigs, the same animals were still interbreeding with boars for many, many centuries. So inside that tame farmyard pig, happily rooting around in its sty and waiting to have its back scratched, there may well still be a fierce, cunning, wily wild pig, just waiting for its chance to reemerge!

WHERE IT ALL BEGAN

Pigs were first domesticated from wild boars (*Sus scrofa*, to give their Latin name) in the Middle East, around the basin of the Tigris River, some 8,000 to 10,000 years ago. At around the same time, pigs were also domesticated by the first farmers in China. In fact, the pig may have been the first livestock animal domesticated by our ancestors.

A WELL-ROUNDED DIET

Pigs, like us, are omnivores. This means they can eat just about anything, happily foraging all day long for roots, leaves, flowers, nuts, and fruit—with the occasional beetle or egg thrown in. They're very good at looking after themselves. And once pigs were domesticated, it didn't take us very long to discover that they would eat, and so clean up for us, all of our trash, as well.

WASTE NOT, WANT NOT

Because pigs eat everything, they provide an excellent way of not only cleaning up household waste but also turning it into delicious pork! In many cultures in Europe, the Far East, and both North and South America, this meant pigs were prized; in others in the Middle East and India, the fact that pigs eat everything, even dead animals or (gulp) human feces, led to them be regarded as unfit to eat.

SCRATCH
SCRATCH

The idea of recycling excrement might seem less than appealing to us today, but, in fact, many animals, including rabbits, guinea pigs, and baby koalas, eat their own droppings to extract maximum nutrition from their diets. Because of how easy and efficient they are to feed, pigs, in China and other parts of Asia, as well as throughout Europe, rapidly became an essential part of our lives.

THE FACTS OF LIFE

Female pigs, or sows, are also known as gilts when they are young. Gilts can breed at as young as three months old, although five to six months is usual. Male pigs, or boars, mature at about six months too.

A sow comes into heat, or estrus, when she is ready for mating, every eighteen to twenty-four days.
A sow ready to be mated is said to be "hogging."

Nose-to-nose contact with a boar will expose the sow to pheromones—chemical messages—in the boar's saliva and help boost the chances of mating successfully.

I LOVE YOUR SMELL!

Boar saliva contains a very strong-smelling, musky chemical called androstenone. Oddly enough, truffles, a delicious edible fungus, also smell like androstenone, which is why pigs make such good and determined truffle hunters!

Pigs are naturally very straightforward about letting each other know when they are ready to mate: a sow will often stand particularly stiffly and may move her tail out of the way.

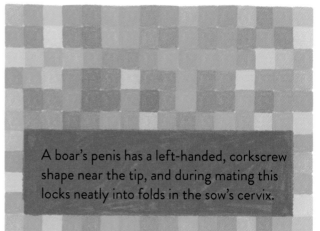

A boar's penis has a left-handed, corkscrew shape near the tip, and during mating this locks neatly into folds in the sow's cervix.

Piglets are born about three months, three weeks, and three days after mating, in litters of seven to twelve. This is why farmers value pigs—a cow will produce only one calf in nine months, but a sow can produce a dozen piglets within only four.

Intriguingly, the piglets themselves produce the hormones to let a sow know to go into labor. The largest litter ever recorded was thirty-six piglets, born to Sow 570, who was part of an intensive breeding program in the United Kingdom in 1993.

1 WEEK	8 WEEKS	10 WEEKS +
A piglet can double its weight in a week. Between birth and weaning, a piglet is known as a sucker.	Piglets are naturally weaned at eight to twelve weeks, after which they are known as weaners.	They then go on to be what are known as growers, or fatteners.
SUCKER	WEANER	FATTENER

In the wild, pigs usually don't live much past eight years of age, but domesticated pigs or pigs kept as pets can live to be twenty— or more. The record holder is Ernestine, a pet pig from Alberta, Canada, who died in 2014 at the ripe old age of twenty-three.

THE SCIENCE OF SUCKLING

About a day before giving birth, the sow will build a carefully arranged nest of soft material. The nest protects the piglets and will be built away from the rest of the herd.

Piglets can nurse within minutes of being born and will nurse every hour if they can. Each piglet finds its own teat, which it returns to for every feed.

They push at the teat with their snout, just as a kitten will knead at a nursing cat to stimulate the flow of milk.

GRUNT GRUNT GRUNT GRU GRUNT GRU

GRUNT GRU

GRUNT GRUNT

GRUNT GRUNT

Sow and piglets grunt continuously as the piglets feed, and the volume of noise the piglets make, along with the amount of nuzzling and suckling at each teat, regulates the amount milk produced next time.

GRU

In the wild, sows hide their piglets very diligently until they are about a week old and start to follow her as she forages for food. In some intensive farming systems, piglets may be taken from the sow as young as five days old. On farms that care for the pig's welfare, piglets stay with the sow for around eight weeks.

GRU

Pigs usually have twelve to fourteen teats, and the first few produce the most milk—a piglet at the end of the line of teats may get less milk and remain smaller (a runt).

GRUNT GRU

GRUNT

19

YOUNG AND OLD

We all know that baby pigs are called piglets, but do you know what a "pig of the sounder" is? How old is an "old boar," and how old do you have to be to count as a "grand old boar"? When would you call a pig a "squeaker," and what is a "suckling pig"? Names for these—and pigs of all ages—below!

A barrow is a young male pig that has been castrated; a shoat is a young pig heavy enough to be ready for market.

SHOAT

A gilt is a young sow that has never had a litter, or that is pregnant with her first.

GILT

BARROW

A sounder is a group of pigs, wild or domestic, and a pig of the sounder is a young adult, about two years old.

SOUNDER

BOAR

A boar is a mature male pig.

A squeaker is a wild
boar up to the age of
ten months.

SQUEAKER

An old boar must be six years
old. A grand old boar is seven
years old or more.

OLD BOAR

A suckling pig is a piglet
between the ages of two
and six weeks.

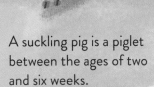

A sow is a mature female.

SOW

SUCKLING PIGS

A runt is the smallest
piglet in a litter.

RUNT

LARGE AND SMALL

PYGMY HOG

The smallest pig in the world is the critically endangered pygmy hog, which can be just eight inches high. There may be no more than 150 pygmy hogs left in the wild, in Bhutan and Assam.

GÖTTINGEN MINIPIG

The docile Göttingen minipig was bred for medical research but is also popular as a pet. When full grown, however, it weighs about eighty pounds—the same as a ten-year-old child. Not so very mini, after all!

KUNEKUNE

The kunekune is found in New Zealand. Its name comes from a Maori word meaning "fat and round."

HOGZILLA

The record-breaking giants of the pig world include Hogzilla, a feral pig killed in Georgia in the United States in 2004, who weighed almost eight hundred pounds

BIG BILL

The record for the world's largest pig has been held since 1933 by Big Bill, who weighed 2,550 pounds—as much as a car.

FROM NOSE TO TAIL

BRISTLES

In the wild, pigs have a covering of thick bristles. This protects them from thorns and disguises them among forest undergrowth.

TAIL

At the back of the pig, you find that little tail. When a pig is happy—if you find just the right spot to scratch on its back, for example—it will uncoil that curly tail and wag it, just like a dog.

TROTTERS

Although pigs have four hoofed toes on each foot, or trotter, the middle two toes bear most of the pig's weight, so these have to be very strong. For us, this would be the equivalent of walking around all day on our third and fourth fingers.

MONOCULAR VISION

In monocular vision, an animal uses both eyes separately. This makes its field of vision much wider to left and right if its eyes are on the side of its skull, but this also makes it harder to judge depth.

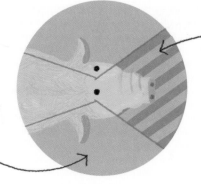

BINOCULAR VISION

Binocular vision is what human beings use. The area where vision from both eyes overlaps in front of our faces gives us excellent depth perception. It also means we can see more of an object if it is behind an obstacle.

EYES

Pig eyes work differently than ours. Pigs can't see as many colors as we can, but they do have great monocular vision, meaning they can see very clearly all the time to the left and right. This helped keep them safe from predators in the wild.

EARS

Pigs' ears can either be upright or folded over (lop-eared). Their hearing is good, so they hate sudden loud or high-pitched noises. And they seem to like music. Some farmers say playing classical music to pigs means they grow faster and don't get as stressed.

Whether wild or domestic, pigs cannot sweat through their skin to lose heat. This is one reason why pigs like wallowing in cool, wet mud. Mud may also help protect their skin from parasites and, in light-colored domestic pigs, from sunburn. Just like us, if they get too much sun, pigs' skin turns red and peels.

But far and away the most amazing thing about a pig's anatomy is its snout.

ALL ABOUT THE SNOUT

THE NOSE KNOWS

A pig's snout is about two thousand times more sensitive to smells than the human nose. As well as being trained as truffle hunters, pigs have also been put to work detecting land mines and illegal drugs.

DANGER MINES

AT LONG RANGE

Feral hogs are able to detect odors from seven miles away and from objects buried as deep as twenty-three feet underground!

ROSTRAL BONE

TOUGHING IT OUT

A pig's snout—which to the pig is like an extra pair of eyes or hands—is strengthened by an extra bone and a disk of tough cartilage that allows it to root through the earth. And a pig can close its nostrils when digging with its nose—very useful!

MMMM, TASTY!

Pigs have many more taste buds on their tongue than we do—up to four times as many. They use their snout and tongue to investigate everything around them and will happily spend most of the day rooting, sniffing, tasting, and foraging.

A LOOK INSIDE

SMALL
INTESTINE

SPINAL
CORD

SPLEEN

SUPERPOWERS!

First of all, pigs are resistant to snake venom—in fact, for many pigs, a snake is simply a tasty snack! And secondly, and even more amazingly, Vietnamese potbellied pigs seem to be able to heal themselves if they develop skin cancer (as they often do). Their cells release antibodies that destroy the tumor, leaving only a small white scar on their gray skin.

BLADDER

RECTUM

ANUS

A full-grown hog will produce six and a half pounds of manure a day. Pig manure contains lots of methane, ammonia, and hydrogen sulfide, all three of which smell really bad—so no wonder pig manure makes you hold your nose!

STOMACH

Sheep, goats, and cows need four stomachs in order to extract enough nutrition from their diet of grasses. But pigs, with their much more varied diet and ability to eat anything, need only one.

DIAPHRAGM   LUNG   VERTEBRAE   BRAIN

TEETH

Pigs' teeth look very much like ours—so much alike in fact that archaeologists have to be careful not to confuse pig molars and human teeth. And just like human babies, piglets first have a temporary set of teeth and then grow permanent teeth after the age of about five months. Pigs can have up to forty-four permanent teeth, whereas we have just thirty-two.

RIB CAGE

LIVER

HEART

Pigs are very sensitive to stress and overcrowding. Some suffer from a built-in panic or stress gene, which causes them to react so badly when being transported in crowded trucks that they overheat and their hearts stop.

TUSKS AND TEETH

Pigs' tusks are the equivalent of our canine teeth. Both sows and boars grow tusks, but boars' tusks are much, much bigger, and they keep on growing continuously throughout a boar's life. As they grow, the upper tusks rub against the lower ones, which are most important as weapons, keeping them very sharp. The very longest tusks can reach one-and-a-half feet long.

Pigs use their tusks for digging up roots and tubers, and boars use them to slash at each other when they fight. In boars, the lower tusks curve over as they grow—in fact they have been known to grow all the way around and form a circle.

THE BIGGER THE BETTER

In Papua New Guinea, pigs with these circular tusks, known as tuskers, are highly prized. Throughout history, warriors and hunters have worn boar tusks as symbols of bravery and strength.

RUN, BABY, RUN

You might not think pigs are built for speed, but you'd be wrong. In fact, pig racing, with young pigs, is an attraction at many a county fair in the United States. In the wild, pigs can charge at over thirty miles per hour, which is faster than any of us can run, even Olympic champion Usain Bolt!

31 MPH

22 MPH

27 MPH

32

LOOK OUT!

Like most wild animals, feral hogs and wild boars would sooner run away than fight, but if they feel cornered, or are protecting piglets, they can be very aggressive indeed. Feral hogs have been known to attack people who are on their own. Hunting wild boar has always been seen as a test of bravery. In India, wild boars were seen as so dangerous that they were hunted from atop elephants, like tigers were. Wild boars and feral pigs are cunning opponents and are known to circle around a hunter and attack from the rear.

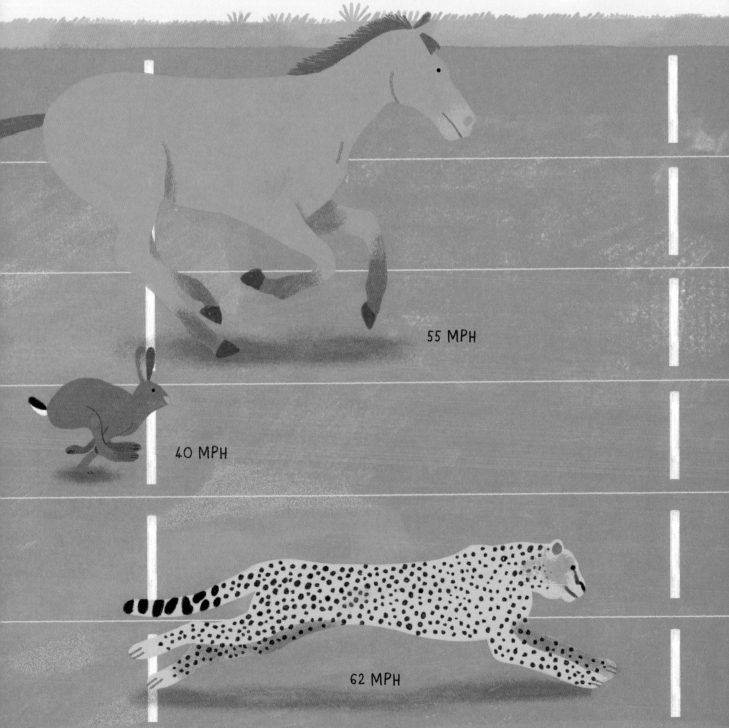

55 MPH

40 MPH

62 MPH

LET'S GO FOR A SWIM

Here's a fact that may surprise you—pigs can swim! In fact, they can swim very well. Like many animals, they do what we would call a dog paddle. Tirpitz was a pig who escaped from the German cruiser *SMS Dresden* when it was sunk during a naval battle in 1914. An hour later she was spotted swimming strongly by a sailor on *HMS Glasgow*. She was rescued and became the *Glasgow's* mascot.

CASTAWAY

Today, on the uninhabited island of Major Cay in the Bahamas, there is a small herd of wild pigs that regularly go swimming. No one quite knows how the pigs got to the island (maybe they swam there!), but they have become a popular tourist attraction.

SICK AS A PIG

Pigs get sick in many of the same ways as people. They also share a number of pathogens and parasites with us, including the bacteria that cause leptospirosis and salmonella, which are as nasty for the pig as they are for us.

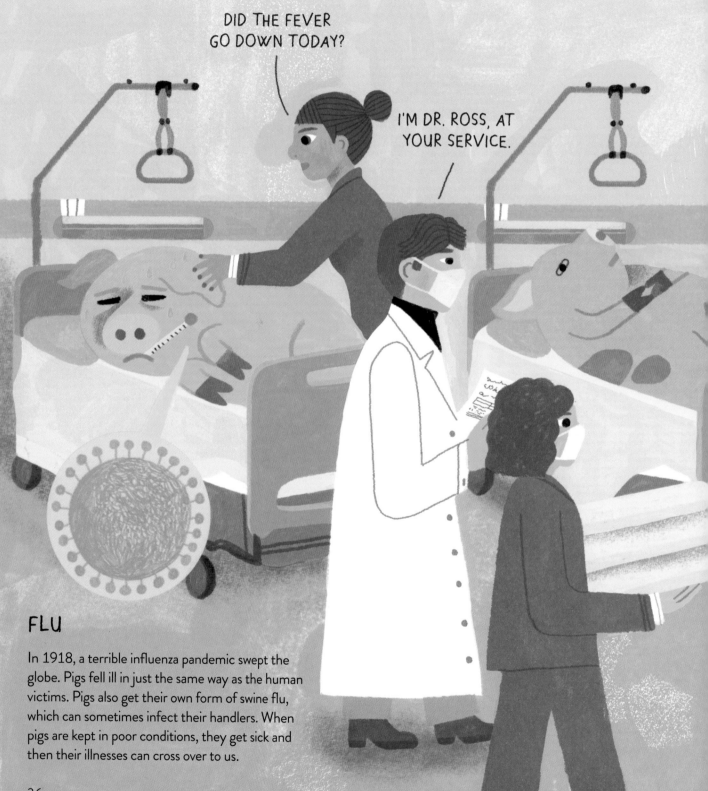

FLU

In 1918, a terrible influenza pandemic swept the globe. Pigs fell ill in just the same way as the human victims. Pigs also get their own form of swine flu, which can sometimes infect their handlers. When pigs are kept in poor conditions, they get sick and then their illnesses can cross over to us.

STRESS

Pigs become very anxious and distressed if they are kept in intensive overcrowded farming systems in pens too small to turn around or lie down in, so they should always be given enough space.

TRICHINOSIS

Trichinosis is a parasitic worm that can live in pigs or in humans—it isn't fussy. Pigs catch trichinosis if their living conditions aren't clean or their food is contaminated; and we can catch it if we eat undercooked pork. It results in a horribly upset stomach.

HOW SMART IS A PIG?

The answer to that question is, pretty darn smart. In fact, they are as smart as dogs, and almost as smart as chimps, dolphins, and elephants. They are very social, they love to play, and they communicate using lots of different sounds, all of which are signs of intelligence. They also display episodic memory, which means they can recall, and learn from, their past experiences.

Tests in laboratories have shown that pigs can understand mirrors and learn and remember new spaces and paths. They react to people paying attention to them and can recognize those they know from strangers.

They also pick out and prefer new toys to ones that are familiar.

They can learn to hold down a lever or button for a specific period of time to get food or open a gate, and they remember which are the best places in a maze to check for treats.

Cleverest of all (and really sneaky!), if a pig doesn't know where the treats might be, it can figure out that it can follow one that does—and push them out of the way!

TOBY
THE
SAPIENT PIG,
From the Royal Rooms, Spring Gardens,
The only Scholar of his Race in the World
THIS MOST EXTRAORDINARY CREATURE

"Learned" pigs (simply, pigs who had been very carefully and thoroughly trained) first became popular in the eighteenth century, but in 1817, Toby the Sapient Pig took London by storm. With just a tiny bit of help from his handler, Nicholas Hoare—a former magician, strangely enough—Toby could spell and read, calculate, tell the time, and even read your thoughts. He also wrote his own autobiography, in which he recorded how he came by his extraordinary gifts after his mother made her way into a learned gentleman's library and ate the pages from the books! A poem was even written in his honor, beginning, "His symptoms of sense, deep astonishment raise / And elicit applause of wonder and praise..."

FOOD ALL YEAR ROUND

For centuries, for peasant farmers and poor city dwellers alike, the family pig that lived in a pen in the backyard was how you survived the winter.

Pigs would be fattened up all year on household waste, then slaughtered in November or December. The meat was salted and smoked to last through the winter months. For some, the Christmas pig might provide the only meat they had during the next year.

The meat of the back was preserved as bacon.

The bones were roasted and cracked open to get at the marrow.

A ROYAL HAM FAN

Bacon and ham weren't always foods for the poor. Queen Victoria had a standing order for six hams from Smithfield, Virginia, to be delivered to the royal household every week, while the famous nineteenth-century actress Sarah Bernhardt had Virginia hams sent to her in Paris.

IT'S GOOD, ISN'T IT?

YES, IT IS!

Pig's blood was mixed with oatmeal and spices to make black pudding.

A whole pig, roasted, stuffed, and traditionally served with an apple in its mouth, has been the centerpiece of feasts and celebrations from ancient Rome to today, and both suckling pig and open-air hog roasts are still food for special occasions.

The head would be boiled and the meat picked off it to make headcheese.

Even the ears and tail could be cooked and eaten.

The legs became different sorts of hams.

The shoulder might become a roast or a pork steak.

Sausages were stored very carefully somewhere cold and dry.

The fat from a pig would be rendered down to make lard, which is where the English word "larder" comes from, for a room where food is stored.

THE INTERNATIONAL PIG

Many places in the world have their own favorite recipes and traditional dishes celebrating the pig. Here are just a few of them.

ENGLISH BREAKFAST

ENGLAND

SPAM SUSHI

HAWAII

BACON EXPLOSION

UNITED STATES

BRAZIL

PARAGUAY

SPAIN

FEIJOADA

PERNIL ASADO

COCIDO

42

PIED DE PORC

SCHWEINSHAXE

BUZHENINA

GOULASH

TONKATSU

ROUSONG

PORK AND PEANUT STEW

KHANOM CHIN NAM NGIAO

FRANCE

GERMANY

UKRAINE

HUNGARY

JAPAN

CHINA

THAILAND

SOUTH AFRICA

SAUSAGEOLOGY

Every part of a pig can be put to good use—even its intestines, which historically were used as sausage casings, and its internal organs, which can be mixed with herbs, spices, and other flavorings to become the meat of the sausage. The word "sausage" comes from the Latin, *salsicus*, which means "seasoned with salt."

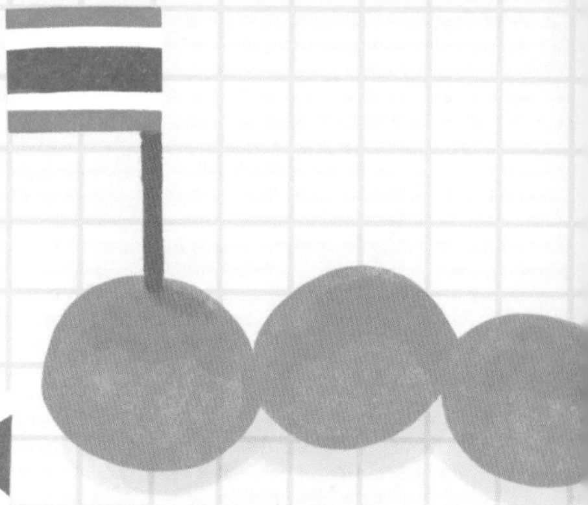

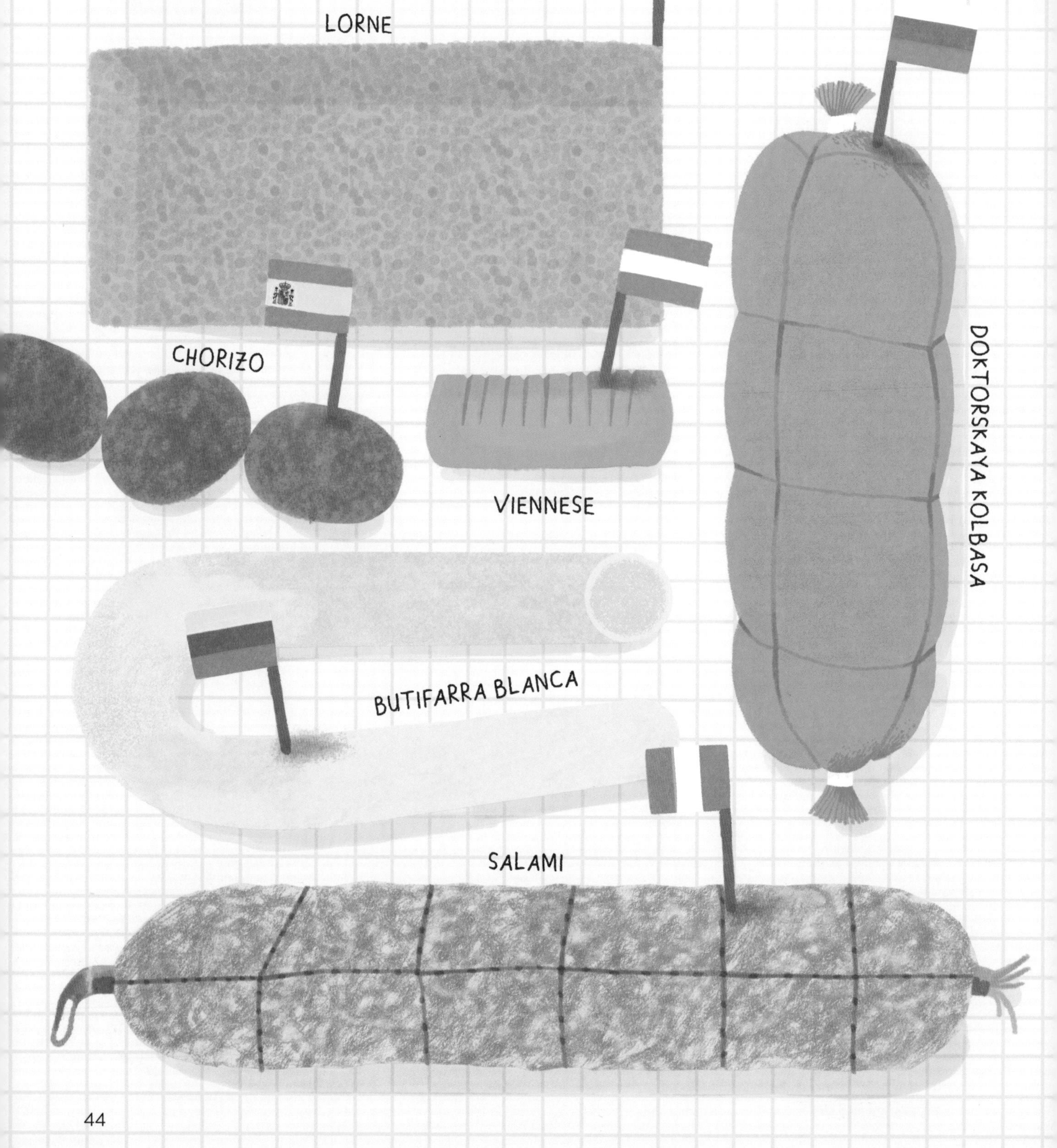

LORNE

CHORIZO

VIENNESE

DOKTORSKAYA KOLBASA

BUTIFARRA BLANCA

SALAMI

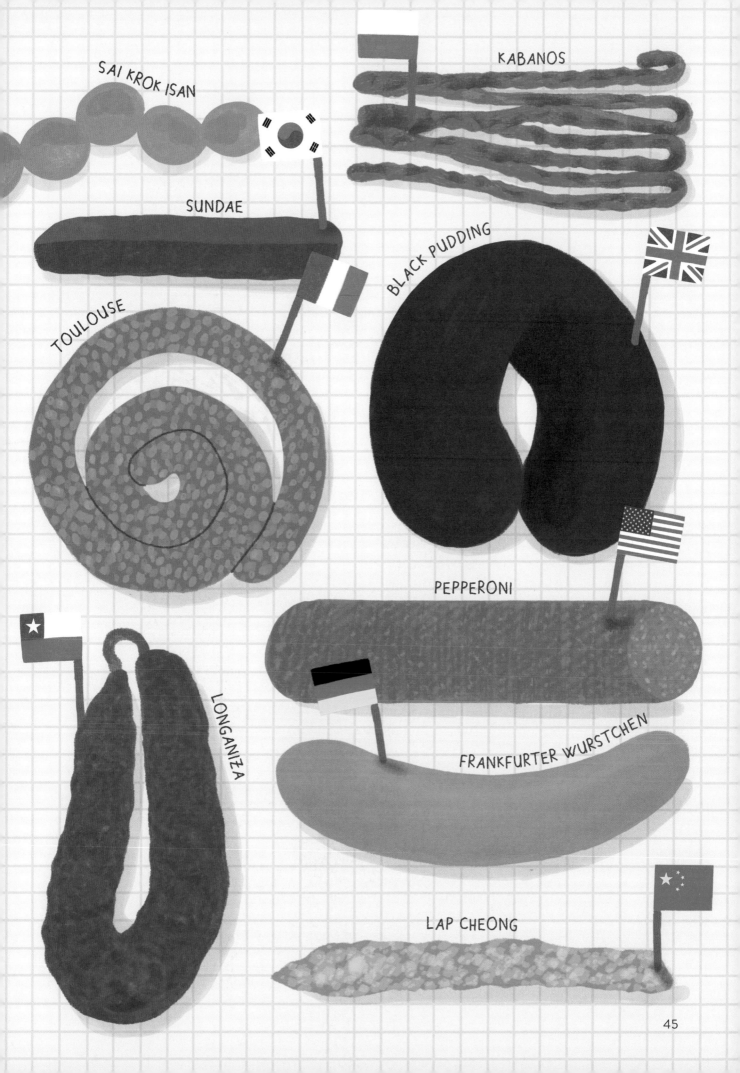

SAI KROK ISAN

KABANOS

SUNDAE

BLACK PUDDING

TOULOUSE

PEPPERONI

LONGANIZA

FRANKFURTER WURSTCHEN

LAP CHEONG

45

EVERYTHING BUT THE SQUEAL

There's an old proverb that you can use every part of a pig apart from its squeal. And it's true—the uses to which we put the pig are astonishing.

BRUSH

Pigs give us pig bristles, which are particularly sturdy and used to make brushes for artists, for painting walls, or for polishing shoes.

FINE BONE CHINA

Ground pig bone is used to make cellular concrete, and is also an ingredient in paint and bone china.

LEATHER

Pig skin can be tanned to make leather, while plastic surgeons use dressings made from pig skin to help treat burns.

FOOTBALLS

Pig bladders used to be inflated to use as footballs, which is why footballs in the United States are still called "pigskins."

VALVES

The valves from pig hearts work in the same way as ours, so they are often used in heart surgery.

GELATIN

The most important industrial product we get from pigs today is gelatin. Gelatin is made from collagen, a protein found in the connective tissue of all animals. It can be stored as a powder when dry, but once liquid is added it makes a colorless, flavorless, gummy gel. Worldwide, we use some 400,000 metric tons of it a year.

TOOTHPASTE

Gelatin is used to keep toothpaste soft enough to squeeze.

CHEESECAKE

It can be found in cheesecake and other cold desserts, as well as in margarine and other soft spreads.

MARSHMALLOWS

You'll find gelatin in the marshmallows you toast on a cookout.

VITAMINS

The capsules for vitamins are often made of gelatin.

PHOTOGRAPHIC FILM

The emulsion for coating photographic film is also made of gelatin.

SANDPAPER

Gelatin is in the glue that holds the match head to the match, and that sticks the grains of sand to sandpaper.

THE MYTHOLOGICAL PIG

Pigs are not only an important part of our daily lives, they also play a significant role in our culture. Around the world there are many myths and fables about them. Sometimes they symbolize human behavior; or they may represent an opportunity for human heroes to test their strength.

A GREEK ENCHANTRESS

In the *Odyssey*, Odysseus visits the enchantress Circe, who serves up a magic feast that turns his crew into pigs. Perhaps she wasn't impressed by their table manners.

MIND YOUR MUSCLES!

Hercules—the strongest man in the world—was sent to capture the enormous Erymanthian boar as the fourth of his Twelve Labors. The boar was not only very big but also very strong—Hercules had to chase it around and around Mount Erymanthos in Greece before he caught it.

GOLDEN BRISTLES, THE VIKING PIG

In Norse mythology, both Freyr and his sister Freya owned wild boars, which symbolized their power over all creation. Freyr's boar had golden bristles that glowed in the dark, while his sister could ride hers into battle, like a horse.

EVEN KING ARTHUR HAD A PIG!

In Arthurian legend, Arthur helps his cousin Culhwch capture the biggest and wildest boar in all of Wales so that they can use one of the boar's tusks as a razor—which shows you how sharp those tusks must have been!

CHINESE ZODIAC

The Chinese Zodiac, known as the Sheng Xiao, has twelve astrological signs, and the pig is the twelfth. According to one legend, this is because the Jade Emperor invited all the animals to a great feast—but the pig overslept and was the last to get there! Nonetheless, pigs are symbols of wealth and fortune in China—even in the afterlife. Some two thousand years ago, during the Han dynasty, people were buried holding jade carvings of pigs in their hands.

SHENG XIAO

The Chinese Zodiac has a twelve-year cycle, with each animal taking a turn. The last Year of the Pig was 2019, and before that, 2007. People born in the Year of the Pig are energetic and enthusiastic—and like being in charge.

WIT AND WISDOM

Wherever pigs have been kept, people have made up mottoes and sayings about them—some of which say as much about us as they do about pigs. For example, in France, if you tell someone they have "the head of a pig," you mean that they are stubborn; while in Italy, to "be a salami" means you are clumsy and all tied up in knots—like a salami.

ブタもおだてりゃ木にのぼる

Even a pig can climb a tree if flattered! It means flattery can make anyone do anything! (Japanese)

PIGS MIGHT FLY!

If something is impossible, you could say, "Pigs might fly—if they only had wings!" (British English)

ZNAĆ SIĘ JAK ŚWINIA NA GWIAZDACH

"To know something like a pig knows stars"—in other words, to know nothing about it at all. (Polish)

LAVAR CERDOS CON JABÓN ES PERDER TIEMPO Y JABÓN

Washing pigs with soap is a waste of time and soap. (Spanish)

SWEATING LIKE A PIG

But pigs don't sweat! This saying refers to smelting pig iron, because as hot iron cools, water condenses on it. (American English)

돼지꿈 꿔!

If you see a pig in your dreams, it will bring good luck. Many people buy lottery tickets after dreaming of pigs! (Korean)

DU HAST SCHWEIN GEHABT!

"You had a pig!" It's what you say when someone escapes a tricky situation more or less by accident. (German)

CAST PEARLS BEFORE SWINE

If you cast pearls before swine, you're wasting your efforts on someone who will not appreciate them. (Originated in the Bible and now appears in many languages)

ГУСЬ СВИНЬЕ НЕ ТОВАРИЩ

"The goose is not a friend for the pig." In other words, be careful when doing business with someone different from you. (Russian)

没吃过猪肉，还没见过猪跑

"Even if you've never tasted pork, you've seen a pig run." You don't need direct experience of something to have an opinion on it. (Chinese)

FAME!

Today, in addition to traditional mottoes and sayings about pigs, there are internationally famous pigs from television and movies. Some were originally created for games and stories aimed at children, but they have gone on to have a universal appeal across all ages and around the planet. There are cartoon pigs, rock-star pigs, movie-star diva pigs, good pigs, bad pigs, pigs from nursery rhymes, and pigs from scary stories. We all have our favorites!

This huge inflatable pig was used for the cover of Pink Floyd's *ANIMALS* album.

ANIMALS BY PINK FLOYD

ESTHER THE WONDER PIG

PIGLING BLAND

MISS PIGGY

PUUMBA

PIGLET

PUA

PLOPPER

KING PIG

NAPOLEON

WHAT
ELSE?

BABE

PEPPA PIG

MCMUG

There have also been famous pigs kept as pets—Abraham Lincoln had a pet pig when he was a boy, while actor George Clooney's Vietnamese potbellied pig, Max, was a favorite companion for eighteen years.

WORTH THEIR WEIGHT IN GOLD

With their big fat bellies and air of contentment, pigs have long been associated by many cultures with wealth and seen as symbols of well-being and good fortune.

In Haiti, the boisterous native Creole pig was a traditional means of paying for weddings…

In the highland villages of Papua New Guinea, necklaces made of pigs' tusks were used as part of the traditional currency and worn as accessories.

In rural Bolivia, the long-haired black Criollo pig still serves as an actual form of currency, and can be exchanged for medical treatment or schooling…

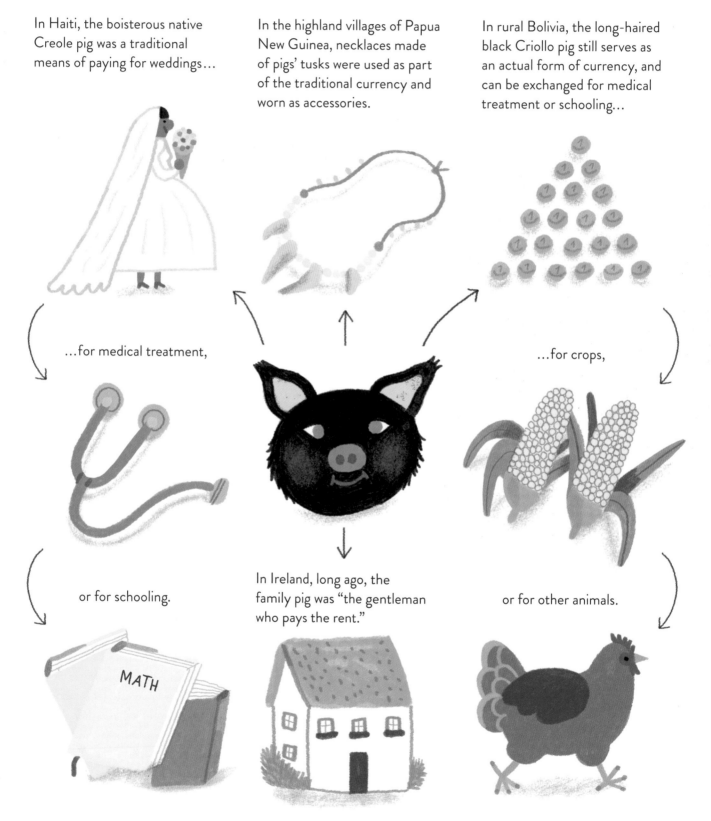

…for medical treatment,

…for crops,

or for schooling.

In Ireland, long ago, the family pig was "the gentleman who pays the rent."

or for other animals.

THE PIGGY BANK

But where does the idea of the piggy bank come from?

The earliest piggy bank discovered so far comes from the island of Java and dates from the twelfth century.

The earliest piggy bank found in Europe was discovered by archaeologists in Thuringia, in Germany, and dates from the thirteenth century.

Some of them are a bit cheesy.

Pygg clay is pinkish-red and, during the medieval period in Europe, was used to make many everyday household items, including the pots in which you might have saved your spare pennies. So perhaps that gave its name to the piggy bank. Or the name might come from the term "pygg," which was used to describe any roundish household vessel. The term migrated over to the United States in the nineteenth century, and piggy banks have been popular ever since.

THE PERFECT PIGSTY

A happy pig will first and foremost have plenty of space—at least one hundred square feet of it.

Pigs need a windproof shelter with plenty of straw as bedding and a means of cooling themselves if it's hot—either by being hosed down, or by creating a wallow for themselves. Remember, these are animals whose ancestors lived in cool, shady forests for thousands of years.

Rooting allows pigs to supplement their diet and keeps them leaner and fitter. Yes, pigs can develop a weight problem, and pigs have even been known to develop drinking problems too, if fed with the mash from home brewing.

Pigs should be treated with respect. Boars in particular need to be treated with a great deal of caution, especially if they have their tusks, as do sows looking after piglets. Being a swineherd has traditionally been as specialized and skilled a role as being a shepherd.

Fences and shelters need to be sturdy—pigs are curious about their environment and are determined and persistent.

In the wild, pigs prefer to create sites to defecate or urinate at least twenty feet away from where they sleep, so the larger the enclosure the better.

PIGS AS PETS

Pigs are adaptable. They can be house-trained and, like dogs, are pack animals, so can create a place for themselves very easily within a human family. They aren't fussy at all about food either! But if you decide to have a pig as a pet, bear the following firmly in mind:

Pigs are sociable animals and can become depressed if they are lonely, so you should really think of getting two, unless you are going to spend a lot of time with it. In which case, consider also that if you do want to go away, pig-sitters are a lot less common than dog- or cat-sitters!

If you turn your pigs loose in your garden, it is in their nature to root and root and root, and they will do so as long as there is anything left for them to investigate. That includes plants, flowers, trees, lawn, and your vegetable patch.

For a pig, your living room or bedroom is just another environment to be explored, rooted through, and very possibly eaten. Pigs should be kept outside.

There are *very* strict rules in most countries as to what you can feed your pigs and whether you can take them off your property. This is to protect farmyard pigs from infectious diseases, such as swine flu or foot-and-mouth disease.

A RAINBOW OF BREEDS

There are five hundred different types of pig worldwide—if not more! If you were asked to draw a pig, you would probably imagine an animal with skinny legs, a big body, big ears, small eyes, and a snout, and you would probably color it pink. But there are also black pigs, pink-and-black pigs, striped pigs, spotted pigs, ginger pigs, and pigs with woolly coats.

IRON AGE PIG

BELGIUM PIETRAIN

MIDDLE WHITE

TAMWORTH

DUROC

BERKSHIRE

The number and diversity of different breeds of domestic pigs today is a result of the needs of farmers in different environments. Some breeds are still associated with specific regions, such as the Tamworth in England or the Gascon in France, two of the oldest breeds in the world. Pigs were bred for specific characteristics. Those such as the Mangalitsa, which put on a lot of fat, were favored for centuries when lard was an important part of people's diets. In the eighteenth and nineteenth centuries, pig-breeding became more scientific, with the introduction of breeds from Asia, which were smaller and faster-growing. Pigs with some Asian ancestry usually have a curved-in profile, with a shorter snout, like the Berkshire. More recent breeds include the long-bodied Danish Landrace. Scientists have also reverse-engineered an Iron Age pig by crossing a Tamworth sow with a wild boar.

OXFORD SANDY AND BLACK

GASCON

MANGALITSA

DANISH LANDRACE

LIMOUSIN

TOKYO-X

VIETNAMESE POTBELLIED PIG

Origin	Vietnam
Color	Usually black all over, but sometimes with pink feet or belly
Appearance	Potbelly, short snout, upright ears
Weight	Smaller types 110 pounds; larger ones 220 pounds or more

Notable features: The Vietnamese potbellied pig was bred for the marshy terrain of rice fields and, as a result, walks on all four of its toes. It is celebrated in Vietnamese folk art and became so popular as a pet in the West that by 2011 there were more potbellied pigs in the United States than in Vietnam.

Fun fact: In Vietnam, these pigs were often kept above fishponds and fed on water hyacinths. Their droppings would fall into the water, encouraging more plants to grow as well as feeding the fish in the pond.

OSSABAW ISLAND HOG

Origin   Spain

Color   Usually black, sometimes spotted

Appearance   Very small! Full-grown they are
              only one-and-a-half feet high.

Weight   Both sows and boars 200 pounds

Notable features: Long ago, Spanish sailors exploring off the coast of North America would release pigs onto any islands they found as a future food source. The ancestors of the present Ossabaw Island hogs came from Spain during the sixteenth century and have lived on Ossabaw Island ever since, with no input from other breeds. They are, thus, living time travelers. The long-nosed, hairy Ossabaw hog is what pigs looked like five hundred years ago.

Fun fact: Ossabaw Island hogs are used to dealing with hard times and can store fat in a layer a quarter inch thick beneath their skin.

DANISH PROTEST PIG

Origin	Denmark
Color	Red, like the Tamworth, but with a belt of white over the shoulders
Appearance	Strong, hardy, and robust, and as its breeders put it, "weatherproof"
Weight	Boars 770 pounds; sows 660 pounds

Notable features: The Danish Protest Pig is a very political animal, with an extraordinary history. In the late nineteenth century, Danish farmers living in what was the Prussian-controlled province of Schleswig-Holstein are supposed to have farmed these pigs as an act of patriotism. Their combination of red fur with a white stripe mirrored the Danish flag, which was forbidden in Schleswig-Holstein at the time.

Fun fact: The original breed became extinct in the 1960s, but in 1984 was carefully re-created to match the red-and-white appearance of the original pig.

MEISHAN

Origin	China
Color	Black with white feet
Appearance	A portly pig with floppy ears and a deeply wrinkled face
Weight	Boars 400 pounds; sows 260 pounds

Notable features: It has to be that face. In mature animals, the face can be so deeply wrinkled that the pig really can't see out at all. With their acute sense of smell, this doesn't seem to cause the Meishan any problems at all, and they are quite happy to navigate their surroundings by nose. But this might account for the fact that the Meishan is docile to the point of laziness—they won't move unless they want to!

Fun fact: Meishan are noted for producing large litters of twenty or so piglets.

GLOUCESTER OLD SPOT

Origin	England
Color	Pale with distinct black spots
Appearance	Lop ears that grow to cover its face, and a slightly turned-up nose
Weight	Boars 600 pounds; sows 490 pounds

Notable features: The Gloucestershire Old Spot is probably the oldest spotted-pig breed in the world. They were also known as the cottager's pig, noted for their calm temperament and ability to forage for themselves, and are associated with the cider-apple orchards of England's West Country, where traditionally they have foraged on windfall apples.

Fun fact: The Gloucestershire Old Spot was the first pig breed to be awarded special status as a traditional heritage breed by the European Commission—and rightly so!

LARGE
WHITE

Origin	England
Color	Pink
Appearance	The archetypal pig in every way; large, strong, and agile, with a long snout and upright ears
Weight	Boars 840 pounds; sows 600 pounds

Notable features: The Large White, along with the Danish Landrace, is one of the most important pig breeds in the world. Both have been exported globally and to this day play a part in numerous international breeding programs. The record for most expensive pig in the world is held by a Large White boar, which sold in the United States in 2014 for $270,000!

Fun fact: It's thought that the Large White may have been bred in the 1850s by Joseph Tuley, a weaver in West Yorkshire, in his backyard. The breed was so successful that it made his fortune.

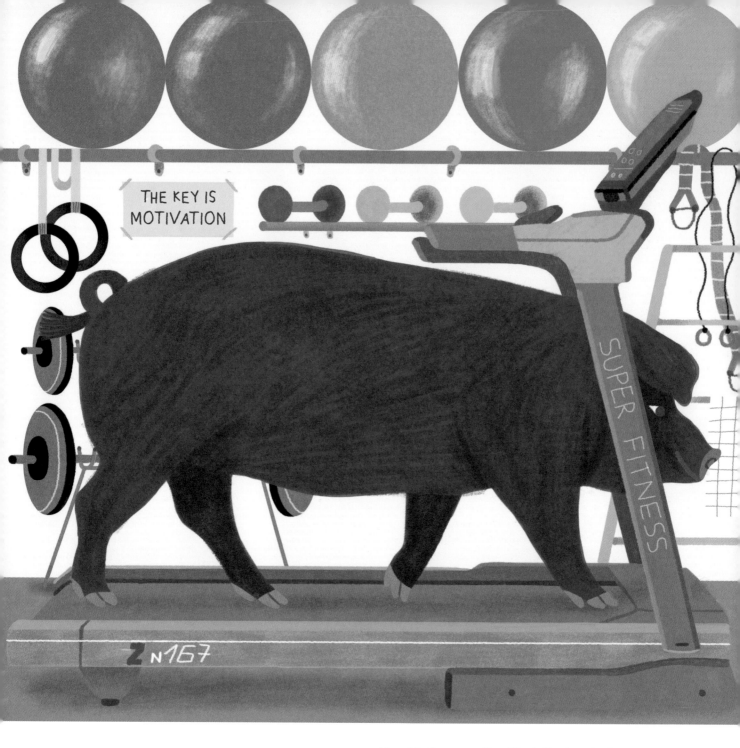

BLACK IBERIAN

Origin: The Iberian Peninsula (Spain and Portugal)

Color: Either red, dark gray, or black, always with black hooves.

Appearance: A lean, muscular, fine-boned pig with very little hair

Weight: Both sows and boars 350–420 pounds

Notable features: The Black Iberian pig forages at large through the oak forests of the Iberian Peninsula (a practice known as *pannage*), feeding on grass, herbs, roots, and, in particular, acorns. Acorns are toxic to horses and cattle, but Iberian pigs think they are delicious, and the oleic acid in the acorns they eat are the reason for the wonderful flavor of the *jamón ibérico*—the most expensive ham in the world.

Fun fact: If they didn't have such an active lifestyle, the Iberian would in fact be a portly little pig—they have a propensity for obesity. Another name for them is "olives with legs."

MULEFOOT

Origin	North America
Color	Black all over with a coat of short, shiny bristles
Appearance	Medium size with a long, downward-pointing snout, like a wild boar
Weight	Boars 550 pounds; sows 440 pounds

Notable features: The Mulefoot is one of the very few syndactyl, or single-toed, breeds of pig in the world. It was popular in the Midwest as a hardy, hassle-free breed, but is now the rarest breed in North America. There may be only two hundred purebred Mulefoot pigs left.

Fun fact: It is thought that the ancestors of the Mulefoot were the pigs first brought to the Gulf Coast of North America by Spanish explorers during the sixteenth century. Choctaw hogs, which were farmed by the Choctaw Nation, have the same ancestry and are also often single-toed.

ACKNOWLEDGMENTS

Daisy: With many thanks to Team Porco: Camilla, Debbie, and Ilaria; to my Uncle Jack, who farmed pigs; and to Mark, who now knows more about them than he ever thought possible.

Camilla: To Stefano, who, most of all, appreciates pigs. To all my friends who continue to be so despite my madness. To Sonia e Tino who are more and more stunned by farm animals. To Team Porco, always!

CONTRIBUTORS

DAISY BIRD is a pseudonym, which is a name a writer makes up for themselves. Sometimes she lives in New York and sometimes in London. She is a *New York Times* bestselling author for her adult nonfiction. For many years she also worked in museum publishing, but now she writes full-time, doing what she is best at—watching the world and dreaming up stories.

CAMILLA PINTONATO is an author, illustrator, and graphic designer based in Venice. She studied illustration at Mimaster in Milan and completed her MA in editorial design at ISIA in Urbino. Her love for pigs inspired this book, but she likes drawing other animals, such as chickens, too. Her books include *Full Moon*, *Detective Mole*, and *Chickenology*. Learn more about her work at www.camillapintonato.com.

Also by Camilla Pintonato from
Princeton Architectural Press

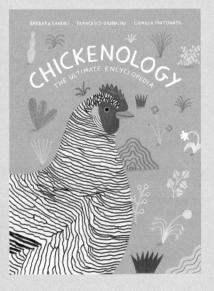